AF342406

THE GOLDEN AGE AND BEYOND

BY JOHN HAMILTON

Published by ABDO Publishing Company, 4940 Viking Drive, Suite 622, Edina, Minnesota 55435.
Copyright ©2007 by Abdo Consulting Group, Inc. International copyrights reserved in all countries.
No part of this book may be reproduced in any form without written permission from the publisher.
ABDO & Daughters™ is a trademark and logo of ABDO Publishing Company.

Printed in the United States.

Editor: Paul Joseph
Graphic Design: John Hamilton
Cover Design: Neil Klinepier
Cover Illustration: Isaac Asimov, Corbis
Interior Photos and Illustrations: p 1 Alien cityscape by Anton Brzezinski, Corbis; p 4 July 1926 *Amazing Stories*; p 5 Aug. 1927 *Amazing Stories*, Corbis; p 6 Oct. 1929 *Science Wonder Stories*, Corbis; p 7 Oct. 1929 *Air Wonder Stories*, Corbis; p 8 *The Thing From Another World* lobby poster, courtesy Turner Home Entertainment; p 9 Feb. 1939 *Astounding Science Fiction*, Mary Evans Picture Library; p 10 March 1963 *Analog*; p 11 Nov. 1950 *Astounding Science Fiction*, Mary Evans Picture Library; p 12 scene from *Starship Troopers*, Corbis; p 13 Robert Heinlein, Corbis; p 14 (top) *The Moon is a Harsh Mistress*, courtesy Penguin Putnam, Inc.; p 14 (bottom) *The Puppet Masters*, courtesy Random House; p 15 (top) *Stranger in a Strange Land*, courtesy Penguin Group; p 15 (bottom) *Rocket Ship Galileo*, courtesy Charles Scribner's Sons; p 16 July 2006 *Asimov's Science Fiction*; p 17 Isaac Asimov, Corbis; p 18 *Foundation*, courtesy Bantam Spectra; p 19 scene from *I, Robot*, Corbis; p 20 (top) *Startling Stories*; p 20 (bottom) scene from *2001: A Space Odyssey*, Corbis; p 21 Arthur C. Clarke, Corbis; p 22 *Rendezvous With Rama*, courtesy Orion Publishing Group; p 23 Arthur C. Clarke at work, Corbis; p 24 *Over the Clouds* by Don Maitz; p 25 Ray Bradbury, Corbis; p 26 *The Dispossessed*, courtesy Orion Publishing Group; p 27 Ursula Le Guin, Corbis; p 28 Philip K. Dick, courtesy Philip K. Dick Trust; p 29 *Minority Report*, courtesy Orion Publishing Group.

Library of Congress Cataloging-in-Publication Data

Hamilton, John, 1959-
  The golden age and beyond / John Hamilton.
     p. cm. -- (The world of science fiction)
  Includes index.
  ISBN-13: 978-1-59679-989-9
  ISBN-10: 1-59679-989-7
  1. Authors, American--20th century--Biography--Juvenile literature. 2. Science fiction, American--History and criticism--Juvenile literature. I. Title. II. Series.

  PS129.H36 2007
  813'.087609--dc22

                           2006012004

CONTENTS

HUGO GERNSBACK

Hugo Gernsback was the founder of modern science fiction. Born in Luxembourg on August 16, 1884, he was an inventor of clever electronic devices, including batteries and radio parts. He came to the United States in 1905. In 1926, he started *Amazing Stories*, the first magazine devoted solely to tales of science fiction. Through Gernsback's leadership, science fiction's popularity boomed, becoming a legitimate and recognized category of regular, or "mainstream," fiction.

When Gernsback first came to the United States, he was very interested in electronics, especially new radio technology. He founded the Wireless Association of America in 1909. He also published *Modern Electrics*, the world's first magazine about electronics and radio.

As a young man, Gernsback loved reading the stories of Jules Verne, H. G. Wells, and Edgar Allan Poe. In 1911, he started publishing their stories in the pages of *Modern Electrics*. He also penned a science fiction novel, called *124C 41+,* in 1911. The writing wasn't very good, but the plot was filled with action and futuristic ideas. He predicted many technologies, which would later come true, including plastics, tape recorders, television, and solar energy.

Left: The cover of the July 1926 issue of *Amazing Stories*, artwork by Frank R. Paul.
Facing page: Frank R. Paul painted this illustration of H. G. Wells's *War of the Worlds* for the August 1927 issue of *Amazing Stories*.

August
BROADCAST WRNY STATION
25 CENTS
AMAZING STORIES
HUGO GERNSBACK
EDITOR
Stories by
H. G. WELLS
A. HYATT VERRILL
JULIAN HUXLEY
EXPERIMENTER PUBLISHING COMPANY, NEW YORK, PUBLISHERS OF
RADIO NEWS · SCIENCE & INVENTION · RADIO LISTENERS' GUIDE · AMAZING STORIES · SPARE-TIME MONEY MAKING · RADIO PROGRAM WEEKLY

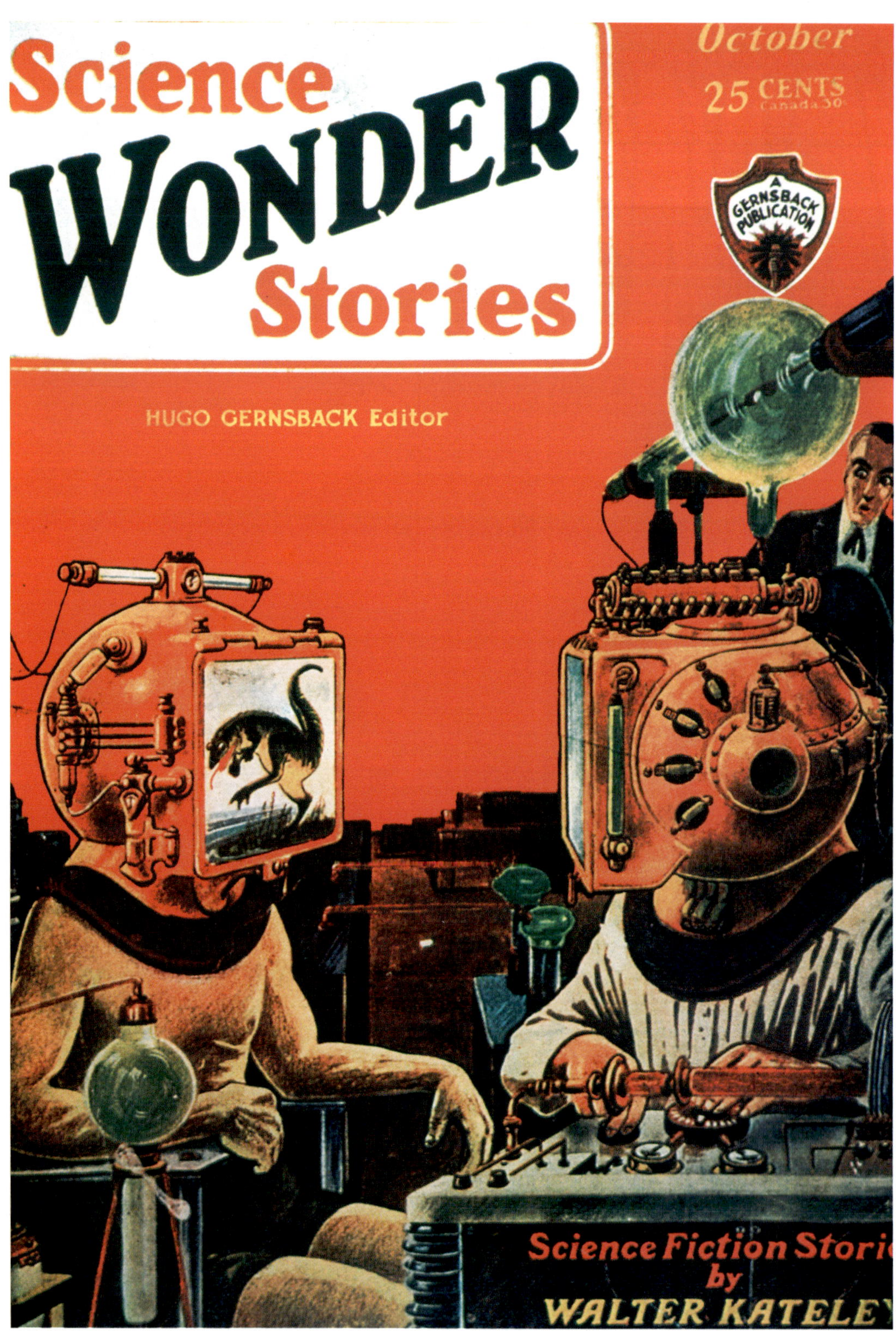
Science
WONDER
Stories
October
25 CENTS
Canada 30c
A GERNSBACK PUBLICATION
HUGO GERNSBACK Editor
Science Fiction Stories
by
WALTER KATELEY

Readers loved the stories Gernsback put in his magazines, and in 1926 he decided to publish *Amazing Stories*, the first periodical devoted solely to science fiction. At the time, Gernsback called these stories "scientifiction." It was a clumsy word, which he would later change to "science fiction." This term, invented by Gernsback, is what we use today to describe stories of scientific speculation.

Amazing Stories was an immediate success. In 1929, however, Gernsback had financial troubles. But he soon started another science fiction magazine, this one called *Science Wonder Stories*. In the years to follow, Gernsback would publish many popular science fiction magazines, including *Air Wonder Stories, Science Wonder Quarterly,* and *Scientific Detective Monthly.* Many science fiction authors got their start in the pages of a Gernsback publication.

Eventually, the field of science fiction boomed. Many other sci fi magazines and books were published. The phenomena that Gernsback helped invent had grown beyond his wildest dreams.

Hugo Gernsback, the man who founded science fiction, died in 1967. Today, the World Science Fiction Society honors the year's best writing, art, and drama. The society's award is a trophy shaped like a silver rocket, and is known affectionately as the "Hugo." It is science fiction's highest honor.

Above: The October 1929 issue of *Air Wonder Stories,* edited by Hugo Gernsback.
Facing page: The cover of the October 1929 issue of *Science Wonder Stories.*

JOHN W. CAMPBELL, JR.

Although Hugo Gernsback was the founder of modern science fiction, the man who shaped and guided it into the modern age was certainly John W. Campbell, Jr.

Campbell started his career as a respected and popular author, but his biggest influence was as a magazine editor. Many of the great science fiction authors of the 20th century got their start after being discovered and published by Campbell. Peter Nicholls, editor of the *Science Fiction Encyclopedia*, once said of Campbell, "More than any other individual, he helped to shape modern science fiction."

John Wood Campbell, Jr., was born on June 8, 1910. He greatly enjoyed reading tales of science fiction, especially the space adventure stories of E. E. Smith. As a student at the Massachusetts Institute of Technology (MIT), he began writing his own science fiction stories and sending them to magazines.

Many science fiction periodicals got their start in the late 1920s and early 1930s, thanks to the pioneering work of Hugo Gernsback and his *Amazing Stories*. Magazines at that time were printed on cheap paper with rough edges. They were called "pulps." Campbell had good luck getting published in the pulps. One of his most famous short stories was *Who Goes There?* This was published in *Astounding Science Fiction* magazine in 1938. It was a science fiction horror story about a group of Antarctic explorers who discover a spaceship buried deep in the polar ice. After digging out the ship, they unwittingly free a shape-shifting alien who can take the form of any living creature. The monster then begins killing off the explorers one by one. Campbell's terrifying story of paranoia and suspense was made into a movie in 1951, called *The Thing From Another World*, and remade again in 1982 by director John Carpenter as *The Thing*. The 1951 movie ends with the famous warning, "Keep watching the skies!"

ASTOUNDING
SCIENCE-FICTION
A STREET & SMITH PUBLICATION
FEB. 1939
20¢
CRUCIBLE OF POWER   By Jack Williamson

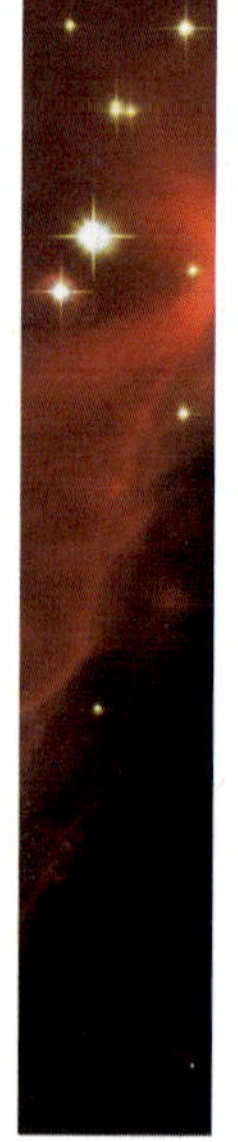

In 1938, Campbell took over as editor of *Astounding Science Fiction.* He wanted to change science fiction, to make it more sophisticated. Campbell was no longer satisfied with just gadgetry and action. Through his guidance, stories published in the magazine began to be more realistic, with an equal emphasis on *science* and *fiction.* Campbell demanded that his writers pay attention to how technology of the future would impact readers' lives.

Astounding Science Fiction became very popular. Campbell printed the fiction of many authors who would later go on to become famous, including Isaac Asimov, Poul Anderson, and Robert Heinlein. During the 1930s and 1940s, some of the best science fiction was printed in the pages of *Astounding.*

After taking over as editor, Campbell stopped writing his own stories. He wanted to influence people. He thought the best way to do that was by finding and publishing the stories of the most inventive minds in science fiction. He once explained to Isaac Asimov, the great science fiction author, "Isaac, when I write, I write only my own stories. As editor, I write the stories that a hundred people write."

Following in *Astounding's* footsteps, other magazines soon sprang up. It was a good time to be writing science fiction. Many people started their careers during this era, in large part due to Campbell's guidance. The field of science fiction seemed to have no limit. This productive time is often called the "Golden Age" of science fiction. After World War II, the Golden Age slowly came to an end, but Campbell had improved the quality of science fiction, making it respectable and opening the genre to countless future authors.

In 1960, Campbell's magazine changed its name to *Analog.* Campbell chose the word because he saw an "analogy," or similarity, between the fiction in his magazine and the real science that was happening all over the world. John W. Campbell continued as editor of *Analog* until his death on July 11, 1971.

Astounding
SCIENCE FICTION
REG. U.S. PAT. OFF.
NOVEMBER 1950
25 CENTS
"CHOICE," by Pattee

ROBERT HEINLEIN

One of the most influential science fiction authors of all time was Robert A. Heinlein. For nearly 50 years he wrote novels and short stories that pushed the boundaries of what it meant to be science fiction. His work was extremely popular, even among people who didn't normally like science fiction. During his lifetime he won four Hugo Awards, science fiction's greatest honor.

Robert Anson Heinlein was born July 7, 1907, in Butler, Missouri. He graduated from the U.S. Naval Academy at Annapolis, Maryland, in 1929. He was never in combat, but his military experience strongly influenced his writing. One of his most well-known novels, *Starship Troopers*, published in 1959, is very pro-military (even though the enemies in this case are giant, hostile, alien bugs).

After his military career ended, Heinlein attended college at the University of California, studying mathematics and physics. He then took a series of jobs, including real estate, politics, and even silver mining.

As a boy, Heinlein enjoyed reading stories in science fiction pulp magazines. To help pay off the loan on his house, he decided to write a science fiction tale of his own. His first short story, *Life-Line*, was published in *Astounding Science Fiction* in August 1939. It was about a doctor, who called himself a "bio-consultant," who could determine the day of a person's death by using a special machine.

From that small beginning, Heinlein went on to publish 32 novels and 59 short stories. For many years during the 1950s, 1960s, and 1970s, Heinlein, Arthur C. Clarke, and Isaac Asimov were called the "Big Three" of science fiction, the masters of their craft.

Facing page: Author Robert Heinlein. *Below:* A scene from the 1997 film adaptation of Heinlein's novel, *Starship Troopers.*

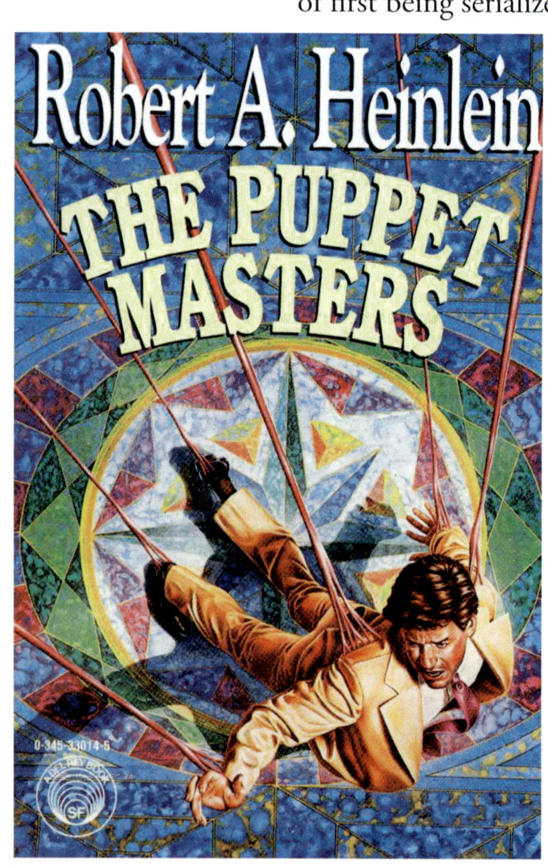

Heinlein wrote a series of successful books for kids, including *Red Planet* (1949), *Farmer in the Sky* (1950), and *Starman Jones* (1953). His most well-known adult novels include *The Puppet Masters* (1951), *Stranger in a Strange Land* (1961), *The Moon is a Harsh Mistress* (1966), and *Time Enough for Love* (1973).

Heinlein's thought-provoking stories lifted science fiction to a new level. Instead of being available only in the low-paying pulp magazines, his work was also published in general, "mainstream" magazines such as *The Saturday Evening Post.* Heinlein was also one of the first authors to sell novel-length science fiction that was published directly into book form, instead of first being serialized, broken into parts and printed over a period of months in magazines.

Heinlein's work influenced many other science fiction writers. His stories led a shift in how science fiction stories were told. Heinlein's characters were not wide-eyed adventurers awed by future technology. Instead, they were everyday heroes who took their world for granted. Heinlein also insisted on realism in his stories. He was aided in this by his scientific background.

Heinlein's work is often called "social" science fiction. His stories, although set in the future, are about things we often think about today: freedom, privacy, religion, race, and love. But Heinlein could also wrap these larger themes around tales of high adventure. He wrote, in amazing detail, about trips to the moon and other planets. In his 1941 short story, *Universe,* he wrote about a trip to the stars in a "generation ship," in which

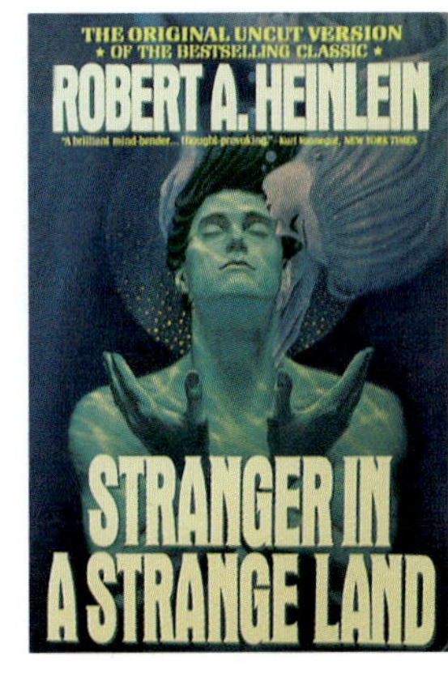

inhabitants are born, live, and die within the spaceship, for many generations over hundreds of years, until the travelers forget their original mission. In his novel, *The Moon is a Harsh Mistress* (1966), Heinlein wrote about a moon colony's revolt against its Earth masters.

When he was at his best, however, Heinlein used science fiction to challenge society. He made people think, and his books became popular with all readers, not just those of science fiction. In his mystical 1961 novel, *Stranger in a Strange Land*, Heinlein wrote about a human, Valentine Smith, raised by aliens on Mars. Smith then returns to Earth as an adult. He doesn't understand things like war or jealousy, or even religion. Smith tries to help humanity and begins to change society through his teachings.

Heinlein was a "didactic" writer; he loved teaching through the mouths of his characters. Through Smith's alien-bred and open-minded point of view, Heinlein questioned much of what we take for granted in society today, including religion, love, and the fear of death. *Stranger in a Strange Land* is considered by many people to be one of Heinlein's masterpieces. It won a Hugo Award in 1961.

Robert A. Heinlein continued writing science fiction until his death on May 8, 1988. Most of his books are still available in print even today, many decades after they were first published.

Left: One of Heinlein's first novels was 1947's *Rocket Ship Galileo.*

ISAAC ASIMOV

Dr. Isaac Asimov was one of the most popular and productive science fiction writers of the 20th century. He was born in Russia on January 2, 1920. He immigrated to the United States with his parents in 1923. His father ran a candy store, and Isaac helped out when he got older.

Asimov was a quick learner, with a great memory. A natural storyteller, he was writing stories, in longhand, by the time he was 11 years old. When he was 15, his father bought him his first typewriter, for $10. Almost immediately, Asimov began churning out stories of fantasy and science fiction. At first, he imitated the stories he'd read in the pulp magazines, with their zooming spaceships, ray guns, and other whiz-bang technology. But eventually, Asimov created his own writing style, which emphasized people solving problems rationally in the face of future events. In 1939, Asimov was rewarded for his hard work. *Marooned Off Vesta*, a story about three men who survive the wreck of their spaceship in the asteroid belt, was published in *Amazing Stories*. Asimov was only 18 years old.

Within a few short years Asimov was selling his work regularly in magazines. His writing didn't earn Asimov much money in those early years, but he made enough to pay for college tuition, and to start a savings account.

Asimov received a degree in chemistry from Columbia University in 1939. He applied to several medical schools, but was rejected by all. He kept studying chemistry at Columbia, and in 1948 received his Ph.D. The "Good Doctor," as Asimov was called by his friends, spent time teaching biochemistry at Boston University School of Medicine. But writing fiction was his first, true love. He continued writing short stories and novels, and sending them away to be published. By the early 1950s, he was making enough money from the sale of his novels to quit his teaching job. He could finally concentrate on what he did best: write tales of science fiction.

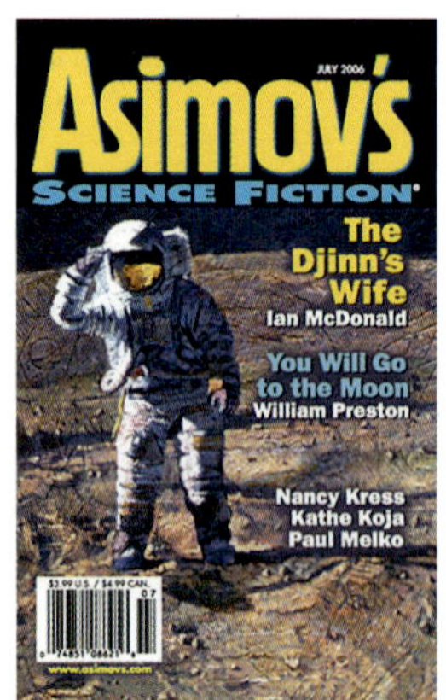

Above: The first book in Asimov's *Foundation* series, with cover art by Tim White.

Asimov led a remarkable career as a science fiction writer. After a span of nearly half a century, by the time Asimov died in 1992 he had written or edited more than 500 books, plus countless articles and essays. He wasn't limited to science fiction; he also wrote many mysteries and fantasies. In addition to his fiction, Asimov had a gift for making science easy to understand. He wrote popular books about chemistry and physics and many other scientific subjects.

As a master of science fiction, Asimov was most famous for a series of related books and short stories about a far-flung space civilization. His epic *Foundation* series spans thousands of years of future history, a sort of Roman Empire in space. The closely linked tales, which contain nearly one million words, tell the story of mathematician Hari Seldon, who foresees the collapse of the Galactic Empire. To protect humankind's knowledge, Seldon builds a sheltered colony called Foundation on a distant planet, with the hope of rebuilding civilization after its fall.

One of Asimov's favorite science fiction subjects was robots. In the 1920s and 1930s, many robot stories told of mechanical slaves who revolted violently against their creators. Asimov's vision of the future was something quite different. He created a world where robots and humans could coexist peacefully. To Asimov, this was more realistic and rational.

Asimov is famous for creating the Three Laws of Robotics, programming code embedded in robots' computer brains that instructed them how to behave. Without these rules, the robot could not function. This ensured that robots couldn't turn against their human masters. Asimov's point was to show that human lives could be made better through a mastery of technology.

I, Robot is a collection of nine related robot stories written in the 1940s and 1950s. *Robbie,* the first, is a story about a mute RB-Series robot placed with a family to be a nursemaid for the couple's daughter. The little girl becomes very fond of Robbie, but the mother distrusts robots. She thinks Robbie is unsafe and dangerous. Her opinion about robots is later changed when Robbie saves the daughter from a potentially fatal accident.

ASIMOV'S THREE LAWS OF ROBOTICS:

1. A robot may not injure a human being, or, through inaction, allow a human being to come to harm.

2. A robot must obey the orders given it by human beings except where such orders would conflict with the First Law.

3. A robot must protect its own existence as long as such protection does not conflict with the First or Second Law.

ARTHUR C. CLARKE

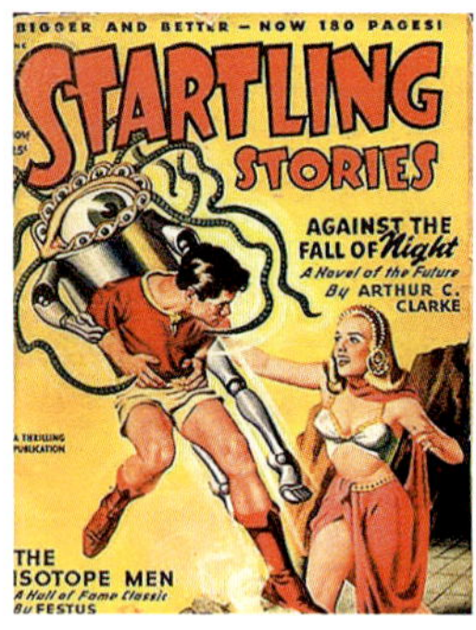

Above: An issue of *Startling Stories* with Clarke's "Against the Fall of Night."
Facing page: Arthur C. Clarke.
Below: A scene from *2001: A Space Odyssey.*

Arthur C. Clarke is considered one of the "Big Three" writers of science fiction, along with Isaac Asimov and Robert Heinlein. Clarke was born on December 16, 1917, in Somerset, England. As a boy, he was very interested in astronomy. He was also an avid reader of science fiction magazines. During World War II, Clarke served as a radar specialist. After the war, he studied mathematics and physics at King's College in London.

In 1946, Clarke sold a short story, *Rescue Party*, to *Astounding Science Fiction*. By 1951, Clarke was earning a living writing full-time. With his scientific background, Clarke's stories are very realistic, with characters who use technological breakthroughs to solve problems. Many of his stories almost seem like newspaper reports from the future. But despite Clarke's realism, his stories are also marked with humor, plus a sense of wonder. Most importantly, Clarke explores a common theme in many of his books and stories: humankind, if it wants to survive, must work together and change in order to overcome the perils and challenges of the future.

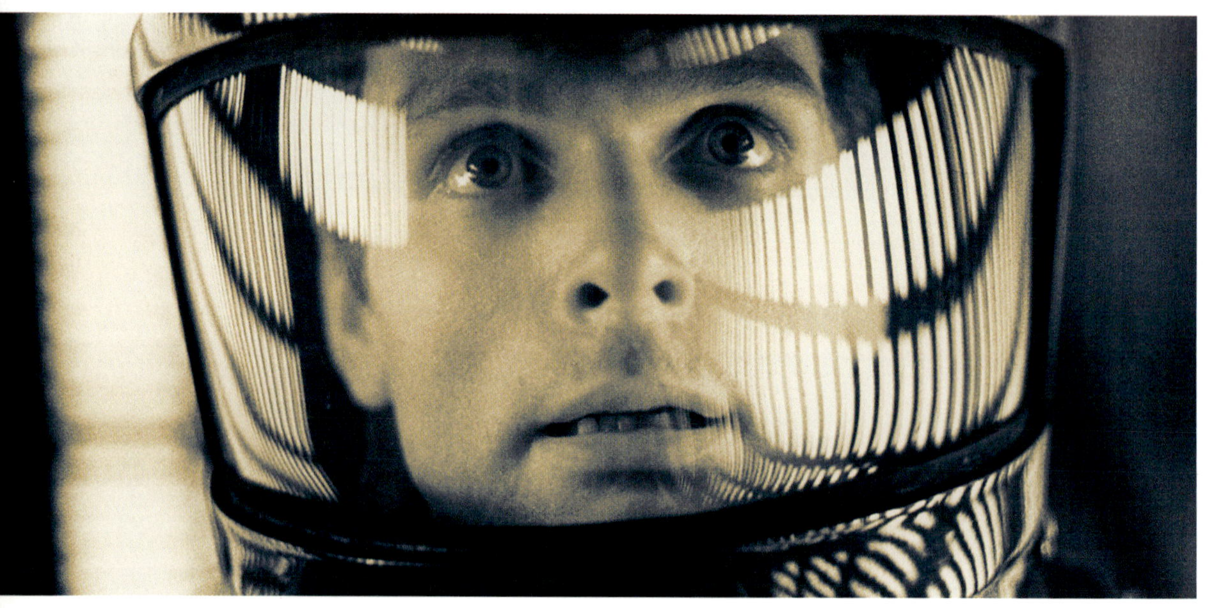

SF MASTERWORKS
RENDEZVOUS WITH RAMA
ARTHUR C. CLARKE
ENDEAVOUR

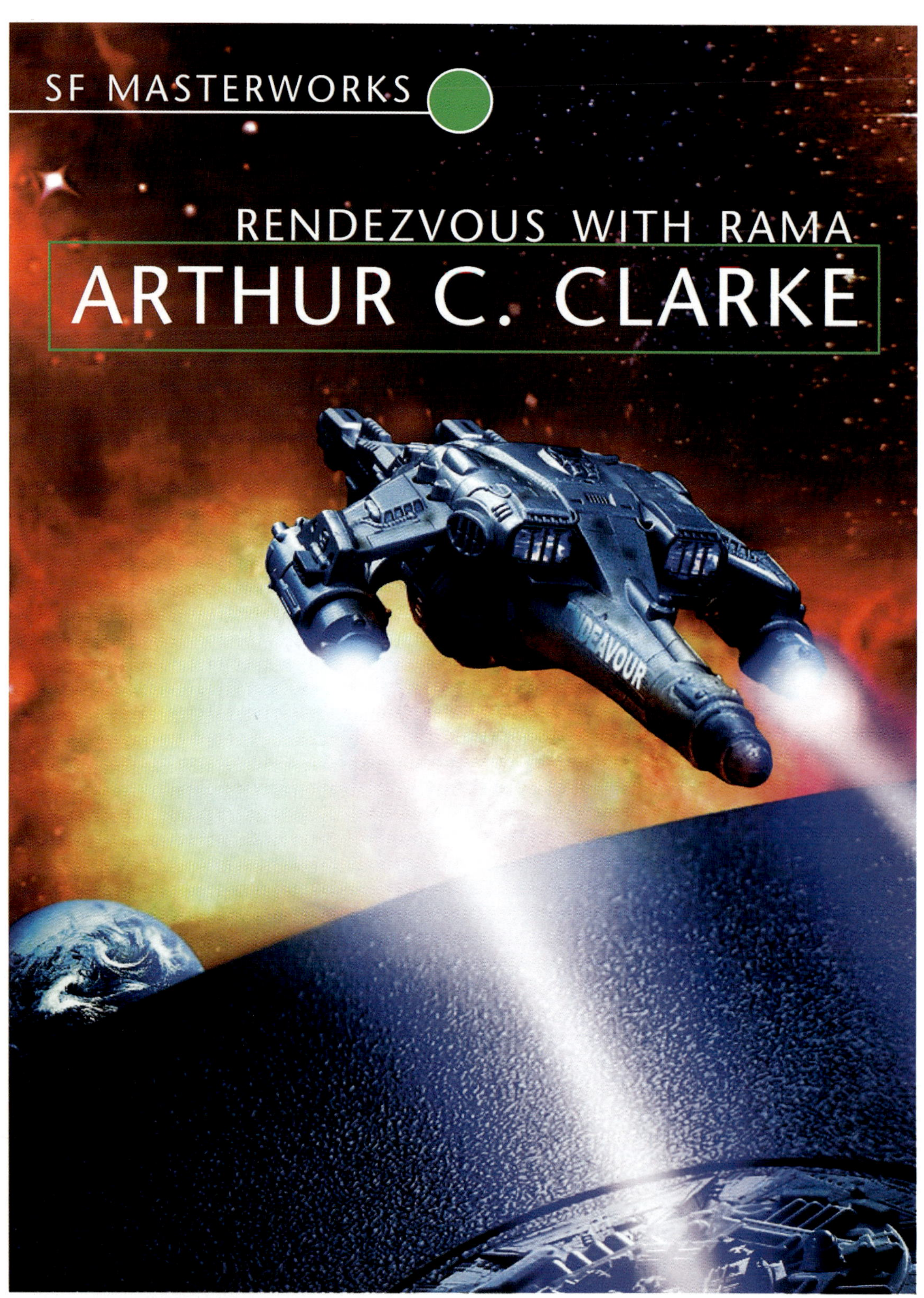

22

Clarke is probably best known for his 1968 novel, *2001: A Space Odyssey*. That same year, Clarke worked with Stanley Kubrick to make a film version. The novel, based loosely on Clarke's 1950 short story, *The Sentinel*, is about a spaceship crew sent to Jupiter to make contact with a mysterious race of aliens. A computer called HAL 9000, which malfunctions during the journey, controls their spaceship, the *Discovery One*. When the crew tries shutting down the computer, it protects itself by murdering the humans one by one. The last remaining crewman manages to stop HAL. Arriving alone near one of Jupiter's moons, he makes contact with the aliens, who mysteriously transform him into a new kind of super-being, a "Star Child" who can travel through space and time.

Clarke wrote about another group of astronauts in *Rendezvous with Rama*. The space explorers are sent to intercept a strange, alien starship named *Rama*, which wanders into Earth's solar system. The ship is shaped like an enormous, hollowed-out cylinder, which slowly rotates to give it artificial gravity. The astronauts go inside the alien craft and try to unlock its secrets. *Rendezvous with Rama* won a Hugo Award in 1974.

RAY BRADBURY

Ray Bradbury was born in Waukegan, Illinois, on August 22, 1920. His most famous works of science fiction include *The Martian Chronicles* (1950) and *Fahrenheit 451* (1953). He is also well-known for his tales of fantasy, horror, and mystery.

As a boy, Bradbury was an avid reader. He started writing his own stories at an early age. After graduating from Los Angeles High School in 1938, Bradbury made money by selling newspapers. Instead of going to college, he educated himself by reading books at a local library. In 1941, he sold his first story to the pulp magazine *Super Science Stories*. By the following year, he was making a living as a writer.

Unlike the "hard science fiction" of Arthur C. Clarke or Isaac Asimov, Bradbury's stories are symbolic, his writing often poetic. He uses familiar science fiction devices, like rocket ships and ray guns, but his themes include moral problems, lost childhood innocence, and how sometimes science, in the wrong hands, can be used to crush the human spirit.

The Martian Chronicles is a collection of loosely-connected short stories about the exploration and settlement of the planet Mars. The native Martians, whom Bradbury describes as superior telepathic beings, are eventually destroyed by thoughtless and greedy Earthlings. Mars becomes a tragic mirror of our Earth today, polluted and sterile, corrupted by human civilization.

Bradbury's *Fahrenheit 451* (the temperature at which paper burns) takes place in a future where books are banned because the government wants to control the thoughts of its citizens. People get their information from government-controlled TV shows. "Firemen" seek out illegal books and burn them.

Bradbury wrote *Fahrenheit 451* as a reaction to American censorship, and to the burning of books by Nazi Germany during the 1930s, shortly before World War II. Bradbury's fear of government censorship and thought-control is a worry shared by many. The book became very popular, not just among science fiction fans, but also by the general public.

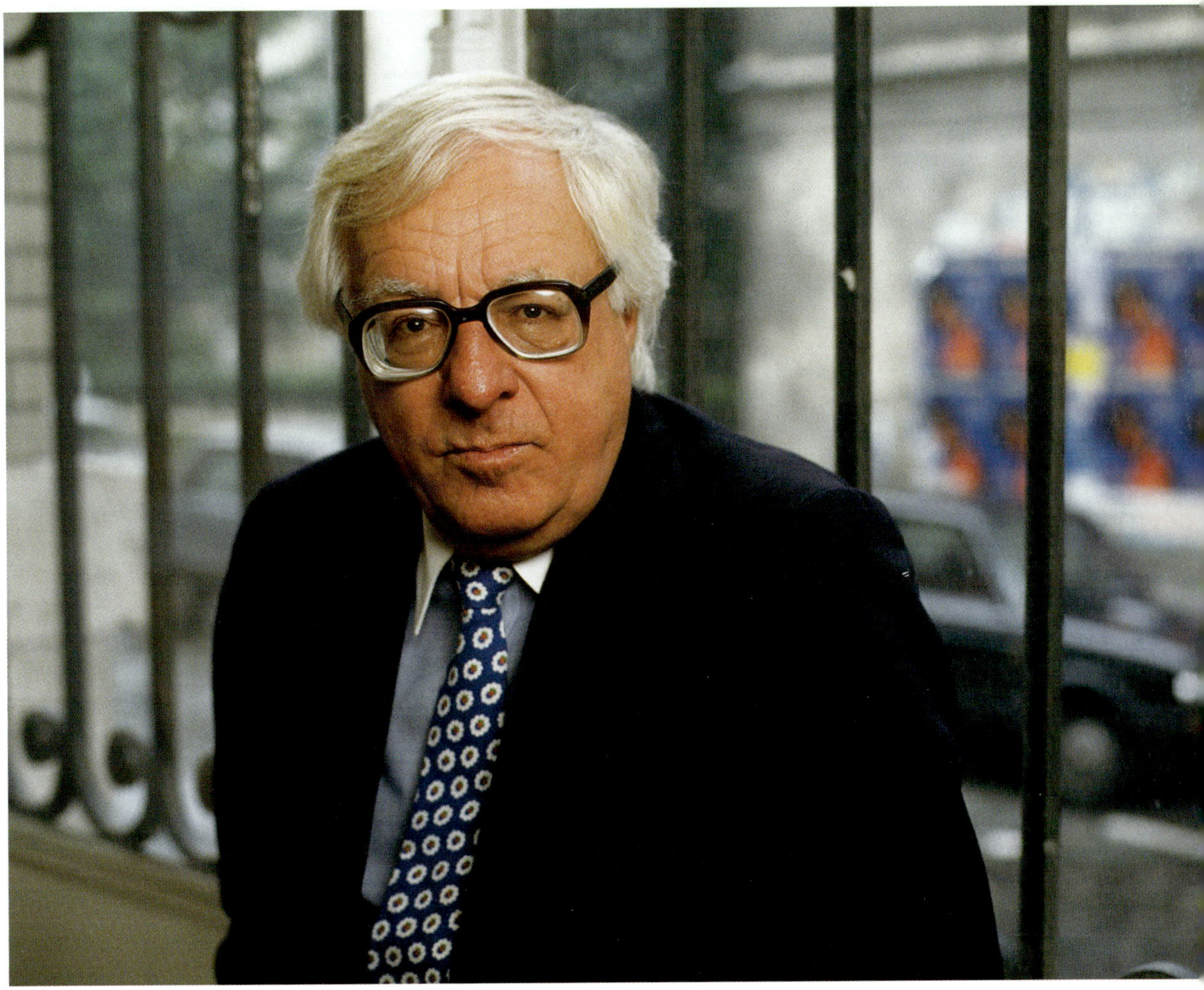

URSULA K. LE GUIN

American author Ursula K. Le Guin is well known for writing fantasy, especially her *Earthsea* novels, but she is also a master of science fiction. Her sci fi books, which explore mind-bending questions of culture and psychology, have won several Hugo Awards. Her most famous novels of science fiction include *The Left Hand of Darkness* and *The Dispossessed*.

Ursula Kroeber Le Guin was born on October 21, 1929, in Berkeley, California. Her father was a university professor who taught anthropology. Her mother was a writer. She grew up in a creative atmosphere, where people talked and argued about a great many subjects, and she was surrounded by a treasure-trove of books and music.

Le Guin started learning to write at age five. She credits her parents with nurturing her budding skills. "My parents," she says on her website, "never encouraged me in the sense of making a fuss about what I wrote or praising my determination to write. They encouraged me greatly in the sense that they believed that if you have a talent, you ought to work hard at it."

Le Guin had an early interest in science fiction. She submitted her first story to *Astounding Science Fiction* at age 11, but it was rejected. She continued writing. After college and a time spent studying in France, she returned to writing science fiction and fantasy stories.

Le Guin started becoming published regularly in the early 1960s. Then, in 1969, she got her big break. Her novel, *The Left Hand of Darkness*, was published. It brought her fame, and won several honors, including a Hugo Award.

The Left Hand of Darkness, like many of Le Guin's books, focuses on a character who journeys to a believable alien world and tries to figure out how things work. The novel deals with gender, culture, politics, and what it means to be "human."

Below: A book cover of Ursula Le Guin's *The Dispossessed.*

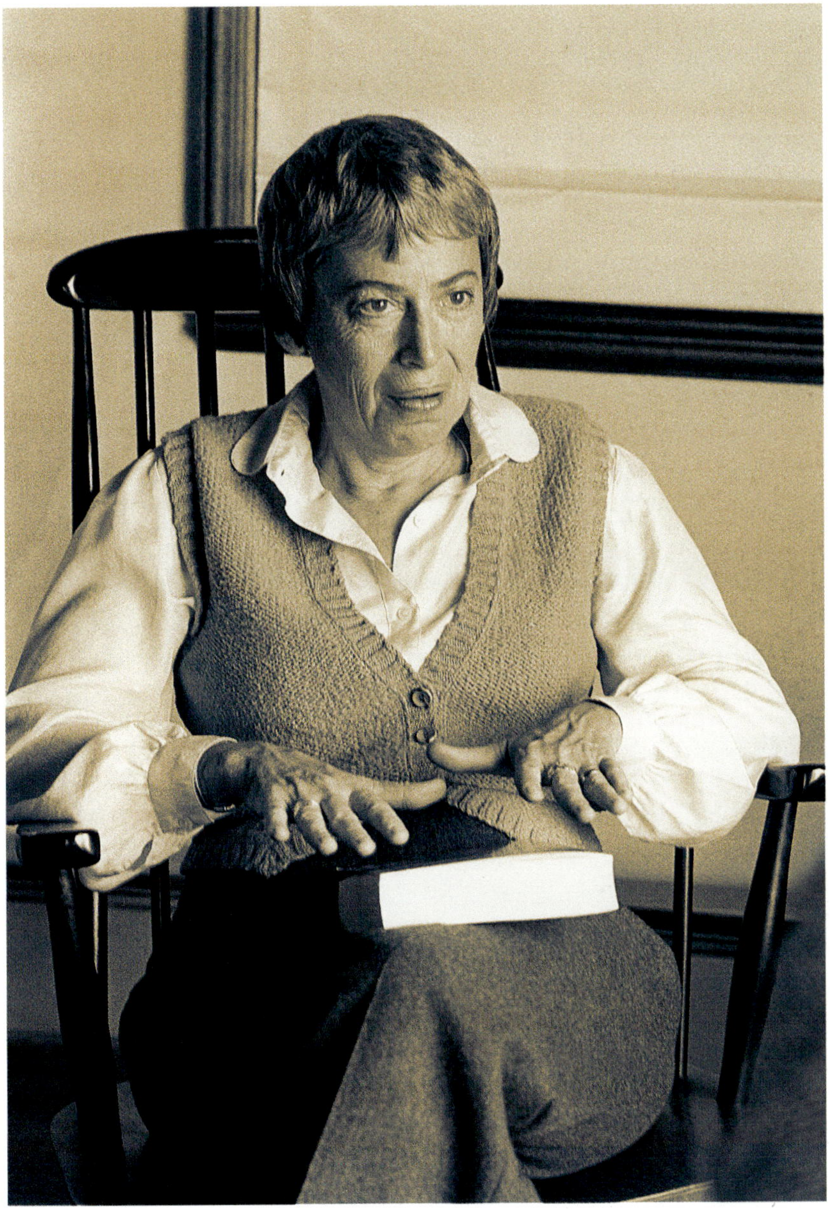

Left: Ursula Le Guin's fiction has won many awards, including a Hugo Award for *The Left Hand of Darkness.*

Encouraged by her success, Le Guin continued writing tales of fantasy and science fiction. After more than 40 years of publishing fiction, her unique vision has found its way into a multitude of award-winning novels, short stories, children's books, and poetry. In April 2000, Le Guin received the Library of Congress Living Legends Award for her contribution to America's cultural heritage.

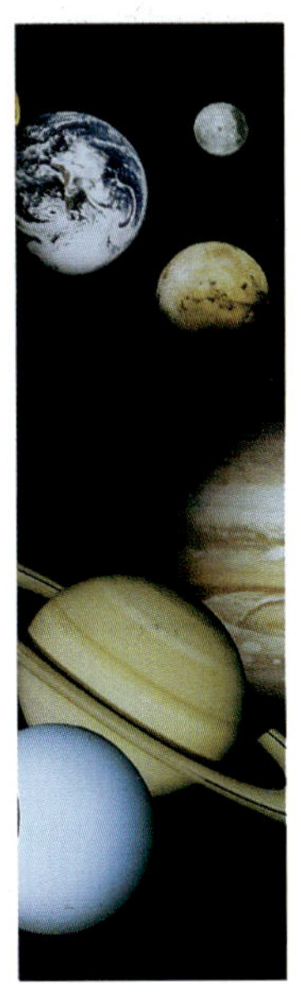

PHILIP K. DICK

What is real? And what does it mean to be human? These are the two biggest questions posed by science fiction master Philip K. Dick. His stories, which focus on normal people dealing with uncertainty and madness, changed science fiction. He was a visionary who foresaw a troubled future. In many of his stories, he wrote about future worlds in which advanced technology strips people of their identities, and even their humanity.

Philip K. Dick's characters wrestle with tough moral questions, such as artificial intelligence, mistrust, and social decay. His books often involve a blurring between the real world and an artificial world, a "virtual reality."

Below: Philip K. Dick's mind-bending stories changed science fiction.

Born on December 16, 1928, Philip Kindred Dick grew up in Berkeley, California. When he was 12 years old, he discovered a copy of *Stirring Science Stories* magazine and fell in love with science fiction. "I was amazed," Dick wrote in his 1968 *Self Portrait.* "Stories about science? At once I recognized the magic which I had found, in earlier times, in the *Oz* books—this magic now coupled not with magic wands but with science."

Dick went on to study many kinds of books, including literature, history, and great works of philosophy. He wrote several mainstream books. But it was his science fiction for which he is most remembered. The genre held an important mix of magic and science that Dick knew would help him express the kinds of stories he needed to tell.

Dick was a troubled genius who wrestled with mental instability most of his life, but he was a very productive writer. He penned a multitude of short stories published in the pulp magazines in the 1950s and 1960s, and dozens of award-winning novels. One of his most highly praised novels was *The Man in the High Castle*, which won a Hugo Award in 1963.

Philip K. Dick's astonishing career was cut short by a stroke in 1982. Sadly, he died just a few months before the release of *Blade Runner*, the film version of his novel *Do Androids Dream of Electric Sheep?* The movie gave Dick long-overdue public recognition and reignited an interest in his stories. Today, several movies have been made based on his novels, including *Total Recall*, *Minority Report*, and *A Scanner Darkly*.

Below: A book cover of Philip K. Dick's *Minority Report.*

GLOSSARY

ANDROID

A kind of robot that mimics people, both in appearance and behavior. In the film *Blade Runner*, based on Philip K. Dick's *Do Androids Dream of Electric Sheep?*, replicants are a type of android.

ARTIFICIAL INTELLIGENCE

A computer that is so advanced that it mimics human thought. Also referred to as AI.

CENSORSHIP

The practice of officially examining literature or multimedia works, such as books and movies, and removing anything that is declared offensive or unacceptable.

EARTHLING

An inhabitant of the planet Earth. In science fiction, an alien might call a human being an Earthling.

GALAXY

A system of millions, or even hundreds of billions, of stars and planets, clustered together in a distinct shape, like a spiral or ellipse. Our Earth is located within the Milky Way Galaxy.

GENRE

A type, or kind, of a work of art. In literature, a genre is distinguished by a common subject, theme, or style. Some genres include science fiction, fantasy, and mystery.

HUGO

The annual award presented by the World Science Fiction Society to honor the year's best science fiction. Named after the legendary writer and editor Hugo Gernsback, who founded *Amazing Stories* in 1926.

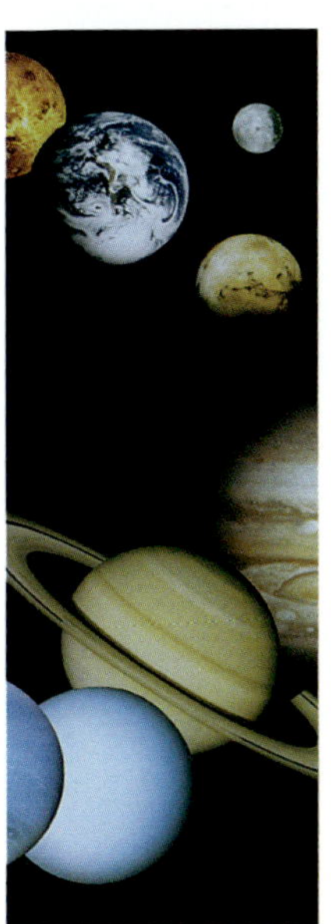

MAINSTREAM FICTION

A category of fiction that is popular with a broad group of readers. Mainstream books have a larger, wider audience than genre books, which are intended for readers with specific interests, such as science fiction. Sometimes a genre novel attracts mainstream reader interest, such as Robert Heinlein's *Stranger in a Strange Land.*

PARANOIA

A fear, or suspicion, of people or their actions, even when there's no direct evidence of harm. In the mid-20th century, many Americans felt paranoia about Communist countries, such as the former Soviet Union and China. This fear showed up in the kinds of movies people liked to watch, especially science fiction films about sneaky invading aliens. A good example is *The Thing From Another World.*

PERIODICAL

A newspaper or magazine that is published in regular intervals, such as daily or monthly. Much of the early science fiction of the 1930s and 1940s was published in periodicals, usually monthly magazines.

SOLAR SYSTEM

A collection of planets, asteroids, and comets that orbit a star. Earth's solar system includes nine recognized planets (Mercury, Venus, Earth, Mars, Jupiter, Saturn, Uranus, Neptune, and Pluto).

SPECULATION

To guess, or form a theory, about what will happen, without firm evidence. Science fiction is often called speculative fiction, because its authors are making guesses about the future, usually based on trends they see happening today.

TELEPATHY

The communication of thoughts or ideas by means other than the known senses. Often called "mind reading."

INDEX